Language Handbook Answer Key

Grade 3

Printed in the United States of America

ISBN 0-15-326162-5

1 2 3 4 5 6 7 8 9 10   170   10 09 08 07 06 05 04 03 02 01

Harcourt

Orlando   Boston   Dallas   Chicago   San Diego

Visit *The Learning Site!*
www.harcourtschool.com

CONTENTS

GRAMMAR, USAGE, AND MECHANICS

ADDITIONAL PRACTICE

Grammar, Usage, and Mechanics

Page 79

1. not a sentence
2. sentence
3. sentence
4. not a sentence
5. sentence
6. Buster has a notebook.
7. Did you like Buster's story?
8. I enjoyed his story very much.
9. Tell me about it.

Page 80

1. *Responses will vary. Possible response is given.* Arthur decided to make lemonade.
2. It was too sour.
3. They added more sugar.
4. They added ice.
5. D.W. stirred the lemonade again.

6-8. *Responses will vary. Possible responses are given.*

6. Arthur tasted the lemonade.
7. Finally, it tasted just right.
8. They offered some to Arthur's mother.

REVIEW

Page 81

1-5. *Responses will vary. Possible responses are given.*

1. D.W. didn't like the first story.
2. sentence
3. The second story was very funny.
4. sentence
5. The other children liked Arthur's puppy story.
6. I always wanted a dog.

7. Arthur opened a pet business.
8. It was a lot of work.
9. Did Arthur lose a dog?
10. He kept one of the puppies.

STATEMENTS AND QUESTIONS

Page 82

1. Do you jump rope? question
2. I like to jump rope. statement
3. Here are two ropes. statement
4. How many times did you jump? question
5. I won the game. statement
6. statement; Are the girls jumping rope?
7. question; The twins are playing.
8. question; We can play Double Dutch.
9. statement; Will Tanya turn the rope?
10. question; Mandy is a great jumper.

Page 83

1. ?
2. .
3. .

4-6. *Responses will vary. Possible responses are given.*

4. How did you do that?
5. I used one of my magnets.
6. Colleen was happy to get her key back.

REVIEW

Page 84

1-6. *Responses will vary. Possible responses are given.*

1. The boys kept kicking the can.
2. The smell of chicken soup was in the hall.
3. A magnet was stuck on the refrigerator.
4. I heard a baby laughing.
5. Marta pulled the string up.
6. I just finished my homework.
7. Marta's family moved.

8. Rosa kept her side of the room clean.
9. Did Marta bring her collections with her?
10. Rosa has a new friend.
11. Will Marta make some new friends?
12. Her new neighbors are very nice.

COMMANDS AND EXCLAMATIONS

Page 85

1. command; Feed that duck some crumbs.
2. exclamation; What a loud quack it has!
3. exclamation; How pretty its feathers are!
4. command; Please take its picture.
5. exclamation; Wow, it's flapping its wings!
6. Hold this snake carefully.
7. What a loud hiss it makes!
8. Be gentle with it.
9. What soft skin snakes have!
10. Put it back into the weeds.

Page 86

1. Ronald: What a good time I had! exclamation
2. Father: Please help me load the car. command
3. Father: Get in the car, everyone. command
4. Aunt Ruth: My, what a long trip it is! exclamation
5. Mother: Look at the map, Ronald. command
6. Ronald: Hooray, I see our town! exclamation

7-10. *Responses will vary.*

REVIEW

Page 87

Responses will vary for 1, 3, and 4. Possible responses are given.

1. The camping trip was fun.
2. sentence

3. We gave the duck a cracker.
4. I practiced my song.
5. sentence
6. I surprised two rabbits in the field. statement
7. Are there many rabbits here? question
8. Shoo them away, Dave. command
9. How floppy their ears look! exclamation
10. Please carry my pail for me. command

SUBJECTS AND PREDICATES

Page 88

1. Allie's house
2. Mr. Puchinsky
3. He
4. A fire captain
5. Allie's father
6. The firefighters
7. barks at Allie
8. gives him a biscuit
9. like Domino
10. is friendly and helpful
11. plays with the children at the playground
12. hides under a car

Page 89

1. subject: I; predicate: love my new basketball
2. subject: You; predicate: are the best father in the world
3. subject: My friends; predicate: practiced in the park today
4. subject: Everybody; predicate: had a good time
5. subject: That brand-new basketball; predicate: got a real workout

6-10. *Responses will vary. Possible responses are given.*

6. Basketball is fun to play.
7. My father gave me a basketball.
8. I watched games on the television.
9. We went to a professional game.
10. A good athlete practices a lot.

Page 90

1. Allie bounced the ball on the sidewalk.
2. What a nice sound it makes!
3. Can you shoot a basket?
4. Shoot some baskets with me.
5. Allie kicked the ball.
6. She aimed at the basket.
7. Allie's new basketball hit the backboard.
8. Julio liked the game of basketball.

9-12. *Responses will vary.*

COMPOUND SUBJECTS AND PREDICATES

Page 91

1. Amy and her teammates stayed at a hotel.
2. The coach and the team's doctor worked together.
3. Fans, photographers, and sportscasters are ready.
4. Amy, her coach, and the other Americans smile.
5. The United States picks good athletes and trains them well.
6. Amy breathes deeply, stretches, and hopes for the best.
7. She won a gold medal and broke a record!
8. The people in the stands cheer, stamp, and sing.

Page 92

Responses will vary; possible responses are given.

1. My swim goggles and snorkel help me underwater.
2. The shovel and bucket belong to my brother.
3. I run and walk along the beach with my father.
4. I dive and swim underwater with swim goggles.

5. My older brother and younger sister built a sandcastle.

6-8. *Responses will vary.*

REVIEW

Page 93

1. One time she had to be carried off on a stretcher.
2. No mistake
3. Amy, her coach, and her doctor worked out a plan.
4. She kept swimming and won a bronze medal.

COMPOUND SENTENCES

Page 94

1. Gloria gave him a kiss, and he gave her a pat.
2. Officer Buckle thought of a safety tip, and he was excited.
3. Gloria is fine alone, but she is better with Officer Buckle.
4. Claire wrote a letter, and Officer Buckle enjoyed it.
5. Officer Buckle was popular, but he did not know why.
6. The children liked the officer, but they liked Gloria more.
7. The students listened to the talk, and they cheered afterward.
8. Everyone enjoyed the talk, and we all learned about safety.
9. Gloria wagged her tail, and Officer Buckle tipped his cap.

Page 95

Dear Officer Buckle,

    I liked your talk, and my friends also liked it. We knew some safety rules, but you taught us many new ones. We remember most of your safety rules, but we forgot a few. May we send you questions, and will you send us answers? Please come back, and don't forget to bring Gloria!

Sincerely,

(student's name)

REVIEW

Page 96

For 1 and 3, sentences will vary; possible responses are given.

1. Officer Buckle enjoyed talking to the students.
2. complete sentence
3. The students got bored and began to yawn.
4. compound subject
5. compound predicate
6. compound subject
7. Gloria is just a dog, but she is smarter than most dogs.
8. Officer Buckle teaches safety, and he wants children to stay safe.

COMMON AND PROPER NOUNS

Page 97

1. Yuko	sand
2. turtle	Pacific Ocean
3. eggs	shells
4. Taro	friend
5. Jiro-San	ocean.

6-10. *Responses will vary; possible responses are given.*

6. teacher	Mrs. Jones
7. state	California
8. cat	Tiger
9. day	Monday
10. building	White House

Page 98

PERSON
    Taro P
    friend
    Jiro-San P
    boy
PLACE
    Japan P
    Pacific Ocean P
    beach
    Uchiura Bay P
ANIMAL
    turtle
    Trixie P
THING
    house
    Sunday P
    September P
    broom
    sand

REVIEW

Page 99

1. compound subject
2. compound sentence
3. compound predicate
4. compound subject
5. compound sentence
6. children C
    japan P
    The children live in Japan.
7. Uchiura bay P
    pacific ocean P
    Uchiura Bay is on the Pacific Ocean.
8. children C
    jiro-san P
    taro P
    Some children thought Jiro-San was strange, but Taro liked him.

SINGULAR AND PLURAL NOUNS

Page 100

1. photographs P   album S
2. picture S   hawks P
3. wings P   car S
4. birds P   mountains P
5. camera S   trips P
6. eagles
7. holiday
8. hills
9. kiss
10. berries
11. bunny
12. guppies
13. branch
14. wishes
15. match

Page 101

1. turtles
2. eggs
3. seagulls
4. flies
5. beaches
6. Two canaries flew into the tree.
7. A few spiders crawled on the leaf.
8. Three branches fell during a storm.
9. Five flowers bloomed on the bush.

REVIEW

Page 102

1. Aunt Rita took me to a zoo.
2. The zoo is in Chicago.
3. What an exciting trip that was!
4. Has Pablo seen the penguins?
5. Come with us next time.
6. rabbits P   bush S   bushes
7. birds P   perch S   perches
8. cousins P   city S   cities
9. parents P   meal S   meals
10. friends P   day S   activities P   days

MORE PLURAL NOUNS

Page 103

1. woman   women
2. mouse   mice
3. goose   geese
4. foot   feet
5. tooth   teeth
6. child   children
7. deer   deer
8. moose   moose
9. trout   trout
10. sheep   sheep
11. fish   fish
12. man   men

Page 104

1. men
2. women
3. moose
4. geese
5. foot
6. man   men
7. woman   women
8. moose   moose
9. goose   geese
10. foot   feet

Page 105

1. letter C   tuesday P   Tuesday
2. alaska P   Alaska
3. uncle C   nome P   Nome
4. bill P   cousin C   picture C   Bill
5. statue C   balto P   Balto
6. men
7. children
8. cities
9. horses
10. teeth
11. babies
12. doctors
13. buildings
14. deer
15. couches

SINGULAR POSSESSIVE NOUNS

Page 106

1. George's
2. dinosaur's
3. mother's
4. Mr. dePaola's
5. story's
6. author's
7. boy's

8-10. *Sentences will vary.*

Page 107

1. animal's
2. boy's
3. cave dweller's
4. aunt's
5. chief's
6. mother's

7-12. *Sentences will vary.*

REVIEW

Page 108

1. bushes
2. tribe's
3. torches
4. feet
5. Mama's
6. George's
7. babies
8. sheep

PLURAL POSSESSIVE NOUNS

Page 109

1. kites'
2. kids'
3. parents'
4. boys'
5. birds'
6. DeWettes'
7. grown-ups'
8. sons'
9. boys'
10. friends'

11-12. *Responses will vary.*

Page 110

1. playmates, playmates'
2. schoolgirls, schoolgirls'
3. mothers, mothers'
4. families, families'
5. brothers, brothers'

6-10. *Responses will vary.*

REVIEW

Page 111

SINGULAR	PLURAL	SINGULAR POSSESSIVE	PLURAL POSSESSIVE
1. lion	lions	lion's	lions'
2. thrush	thrushes	thrush's	thrushes'
3. giraffe	giraffes	giraffe's	giraffes'
4. butterfly	butterflies	butterfly's	butterflies'
5. fox	foxes	fox's	foxes'

6. zoo's
7. monkey's/monkeys'
8. bear's/bears'
9. gorilla's
10. elephant's/elephants'

ABBREVIATIONS

Page 112

1. Mon.
2. Mar.
3. Mr.
4. Fri.
5. Feb.
6. Mr. Jay
7. Ms. Grey
8. Oct. 19
9. Mrs. Pitt
10. Oak Rd.
11. Aug. 9
12. Thurs.
13. Loon Ave.
14. Wed.
15. Dr. Sanchez
16. Tues.
17. Apr.
18. Mr.
19. Ave.
20. U.S.

Page 113

1. Adams, Mr. George
   15 Myrtle Ave.
   Sept. 5
2. Arnez, Dr. Rita
   72 Pleasant St.
   Oct. 30
3. Bates, Mr. Myron
   320 Lombard St.
   Mar. 1
4. Boyle, Mrs. Gertie
   3221 Holly Ave.
   Feb. 20
5. Coe, Mrs. Ann
   798 Pilgrim Rd.
   Dec. 18
6. Creasey, Mr. John
   624 Beach Rd.
   Aug. 3

REVIEW

Page 114

1. Our playground has new swings.
2. Two of them are tire swings.
3. Each one can hold two people.
4. My friend Carol Ann swings with me.

5. Leo pushes us higher and higher.
6. boys' gym
7. Dr. Fry
8. Sept. 10
9. Sky St.
10. Mr. Otis
11. Dec. 4
12. girls' team
13. ladies' room
14. Thurs.
15. Ms. Babbitt

SINGULAR AND PLURAL PRONOUNS

Page 115
1. I, you
2. We, it
3. You, us
4. He, she
5. I, them
6. He wants a visitor.
7. Ask them for their ideas.
8. Show it to that dog.
9. They learned the rules right away.

Page 116
Dear Rosie,

I would like to thank you for visiting last week. I really enjoyed the visit. It cheered me up!

Sometimes the hospital is fun, but often it is dull. The nurses try hard. However, they have too much to do. Visitors are important. We all look forward to them. Please come to visit us again.

Your friend,
Lisa

REVIEW

Page 117
1. Dr. Deeds
2. Ms. Sands
3. Aug. 4
4. Jan. 15
5. River Rd.
6. Oct. 31
7. Mon.
8. Elm St.
9. Mar. 10
10. Mrs. Luz
11. They ran around the cage.
12. It ran around the cage.
13. The mouse looked at him (or her).
14. The mouse looked at them.
15. They caught the mouse.

SUBJECT PRONOUNS

Page 118
1. She
2. we
3. He
4. They
5. I
6. He caught a high fly ball.
7. We clapped wildly.
8. They tossed their caps in the air.
9. Carmen and I practice hitting.

Page 119
1. I
2. He
3. You/I/We
4. They
5. We
6-10. *Responses will vary.*

Page 120

1. The players practice every day.
2. Coach Lane teaches them.
3. Our team does well in the play-offs.
4. We finish third overall.
5. It pleases our parents and our coach.
6. They are warming up. P
7. We take practice swings. P
8. He watches from the stands. S
9. It seems far away. S
10. She is the most valuable player. S

OBJECT PRONOUNS

Page 121

1. her
2. you
3. him
4. us
5. them
6. Roberta dropped it.
7. Ramona poured tea for them.
8. Beezus tossed the ball to us.
9. Give the bottles to Ramona and me.
10. The baby smiled at Beezus and me.

Page 122

1. him
2. her
3. them
4. us
5. it
6. I can't wait to play with her.
7. Will she share a room with me?
8. Beezus will beat her and me at games.

REVIEW

Page 123

1. Ramona and I are friends.
2. room, and they get along well.
3. No mistake
4. She and my sister

ADJECTIVES

Page 124

1. dry
2. Many
3. thorny
4. red
5. little
6. hot
7. sly coyote
8. huge ladder
9. faraway sky
10. many days
11. cool moon
12. starry night

Page 125

1. cold morning
2. big Bear
3. tiny Roadrunner
4. long minute
5. strong Bear
6. fast Roadrunner
7. sharp stone
8. spiny cactus
9. sad runners
10. best friends

Page 126

1. We
2. me
3. She
4. us
5. I

6-10. *Adjectives will vary.*

11. bright <u>stars</u>
12. wonderful <u>artwork</u>
13. mashed <u>potatoes</u>
14. purple <u>car</u>
15. brick <u>house</u>

ADJECTIVES FOR *WHAT KIND*

Page 127

1. bright
2. little
3. long
4. sad

5-7. *Adjectives will vary; possible responses are given.*

5. The huge owl flew away.
6. The round owl flew away.
7. The brown owl flew away.

8-12. *Responses will vary. Possible responses are given.*

8. sight—colorful
9. sound—loud
10. touch—soft
11. taste—spicy
12. smell—fishy

Page 128

1. tiny, pointed, spotted
2. large, curved, black
3. long, slender, patterned

4-6. *Sentences will vary.*

Page 129

1. great zoo
2. funny monkeys
3. bouncy seal
4. red balloon
5. huge lion

6-11. *Adjectives will vary. Nouns are underlined.*

6. A <u>hippo</u> shared its <u>pen</u> with a <u>bird</u>.
7. <u>Students</u> found the <u>path</u> to the <u>giraffes</u>.
8. <u>Mr. Evans</u> showed <u>Mary</u> the <u>bears</u>.
9. <u>Penguins</u> dove into the <u>pond</u> for <u>fish</u>.
10. A <u>seal</u> splashed <u>Juan</u> with its <u>tail</u>.
11. <u>Jan</u> stopped at the <u>café</u> for a <u>snack</u>.
12. The <u>elephants</u> were eating <u>grass</u> in a <u>field</u>.

ADJECTIVES FOR *HOW MANY*

Page 130

1. eight
2. several
3. few
4. twenty

5-9. *Sentences will vary; possible responses are given.*

5. three; Verna sent her book to a few publishers.
6. five; She revised the book several times.
7. seventy-five; The book will be many pages long.
8. Forty; Many bookstore chains will sell it.
9. ten; It will be translated into several languages.

10-12. *Sentences will vary.*

Page 131

1. ten
2. Several
3. two
4. Some
5. One
6. *Sentences will vary.*

Page 132

1. hot swamp
2. big alligator
3. pink flamingo
4. one leg
5. Many bugs

6-10. *Adjectives for rewritten sentences will vary.*

ARTICLES

Page 133

1. a grocery
2. the sky
3. The story
4. an egg
5. a pizza
6. Please hand me a fork.
7. I am trying to eat an eggplant.
8. It fell out of a cloud.
9. I would rather have an ice-cream cone.

10-12. *Sentences will vary.*

Page 134

1. A
2. The
3. an
4. A
5. the
6. the
7. the
8. the
9. The
10. a
11. A
12. the
13. The
14. an
15. an

Page 135

1-8. *Adjectives will vary. Possible responses are given.*

1. farm—big
2. piglets—ten
3. barn—red
4. apples—delicious
5. chickens—four
6. pony—brown
7. carrots—many
8. noise—quacking
9. a
10. The
11. an
12. the
13. an
14. The

ADJECTIVES THAT COMPARE

Page 136

1. <u>Molly</u>   <u>brother</u>   taller
2. <u>Meg</u>   <u>children</u>   quietest
3. <u>house</u>   <u>stable</u>   more crowded
4. louder
5. strongest
6. more active
7. more intelligent
8. calmer
9. most relaxed
10. larger

Page 137

Adjective	Comparing Two Things	Comparing More Than Two Things
1. loud	louder	loudest
2. crowded	more crowded	most crowded
3. difficult	more difficult	most difficult
4. small	smaller	smallest
5. unpleasant	more unpleasant	most unpleasant

6-10. *Sentences will vary.*

Page 138

1. Molly is the oldest one of the four girls.
2. with their parents in a house
3. No mistake
4. Even the animals live in the house.

ACTION VERBS

Page 139

1. shone
2. fell
3. died
4. watched
5. failed
6. moved
7. hoped

8-12. *Responses will vary; possible responses are given.*

8. The farmers worked hard in their fields.
9. Grasshoppers ate many of the leaves.
10. The wind blew dust all around the farm.
11. The story moved in from the west.
12. Thunder shook the house.

Page 140

1-4. *Responses will vary. Possible responses are given.*

1. Leah smelled fresh coffee cake.
2. Papa fed the pigs and some of the cattle.
3. Mama poured dishwater on her petunias.
4. Leah loved her pony.
5. said
6. borrowed
7. clutched
8. bought

9-10. *Sentences will vary.*

Page 141

1. most wonderful
2. nicer
3. finest
4. more difficult
5. What an amazing auction we had in July!
6. Did the man in the big hat come from Chicago?
7. The family eats coffee cake every Saturday.
8. (began) in 1929.
9. (lasted) for ten years.
10. (began) to fall.

MAIN VERBS AND HELPING VERBS

Page 142

1. (is) dreaming
2. (could) ignore
3. (has) chased
4. (have) collapsed
5. (has) destroyed
6. has
7. have
8. has

9-10. *Sentences will vary.*

Page 143

1-5. Three javelinas (have) moved to the desert. They (have) built three houses. A mean coyote (has) visited each house. At the third house, he (has) cornered all three javelinas. The javelinas (have) trapped him in a stove.

6-7. *Sentences will vary.*

Page 144

1. traveled
2. ran
3. say
4. blow
5. The woman has gathered saguaro ribs.
6. The two brothers have escaped into the desert.
7. Their sister has completed her house.
8. The three javelinas have trapped the coyote.
9. compound subject; helped
10. compound predicate; huffed, puffed
11. compound predicate; saw, smelled
12. compound subject; blew

PRESENT-TENSE VERBS

Page 145

1. makes; S
2. follows; S
3. cut; P
4. The river looks like a checkerboard.
5. He watches the snow on the ice.
6. I worry about the weather.
7. Papa and Uncle Jacob step onto the ice.
8. The ship carries ice to warm countries far away.

9-10. *Sentences will vary.*

Page 146

Responses will vary; possible responses are given.

1. I, You, We, or They tap holes in the ice.
2. He or She skates along the river.
3. I, You, We, or They follow the ice cutter.
4. He or She stops for hot chocolate.
5. I, You, We, or They shiver in the cold.
6. I, You, We, or They run indoors.

7-10. *Sentences will vary.*

Page 147

1-4. *Proper nouns will vary; possible responses are given.*

1. The schooner comes one Sunday in December.
2. Pablo walks down to the docks.
3. Will Aunt Marie make hot chocolate?
4. I plan to visit Maine.
5. have ripened
6. has opened
7. has roasted
8. have crushed
9. The bag smells like pine trees.
10. The sailors trade ice for cocoa beans.
11. Papa carries me onto the ship.
12. Jacob shows me pictures of Maine.

PAST-TENSE VERBS

Page 148

1. depend; present tense
2. jumped; past tense
3. begged; past tense
4. The rider walked toward the black horse.
5. A spotted pony grazed nearby.
6. The cowboy hopped into the saddle.
7. The horse whinnied.
8. Then it trotted around the corral.

9-10. *Sentences will vary.*

Page 149

1. carried
2. cooked
3. flipped
4. fried
5. tasted
6. napped
7. washed
8. The horses sniffed the air as storm clouds floated overhead. Suddenly raindrops poured down. Thunderclaps scared the horses. They pressed against the fence.

Page 150

1. She waited for us at the ranch house.
2. He cuts wood for a new fence.
3. They played games every day.
4. We waved to them at the rodeo.
5. chop, chopped
6. lived, lives
7. use, used
8. tried, try
9. planned, plans
10. care, cared
11. hurry, hurried
12. purchased, purchases

IRREGULAR VERBS

Page 151

VERB	PRESENT	PAST	PAST WITH HELPING VERB
1. come	come, comes	came	have, has, had come
2. do	do, does	did	have, has, had done
3. have	have, has	had	have, has, had had
4. say	say, says	said	have, has, had said
5. see	see, sees	saw	have, has, had seen

6. We came home from the bank.
7. We had seen a $1,000 bill.
8. "That is a lot of money," you said.

9-10. *Sentences will vary.*

Page 152

1. Karen has (had) done many chores this month.
2. She has had to work hard.
3. Karen said she keeps her money in the bank.
4. She saw the new interest rates.
5. She has (had) come to the bank to deposit more money.

6-10. The woman (came) to the bank teller's window. "I (had) a check for fifty dollars," she (said). "Perhaps you (saw) it on the counter. (Did) you?"

REVIEW

Page 153

1. came
2. seen
3. sells
4. said
5. tried
6. done

MORE IRREGULAR VERBS

Page 154

VERB	PRESENT	PAST	PAST WITH HELPING VERB
1. eat	eat, eats	ate	(have, has, had) eaten
2. give	give, gives	gave	(have, has, had) given
3. go	go, goes	went	(have, has, had) gone
4. ride	ride, rides	rode	(have, has, had) ridden
5. take	take, takes	took	(have, has, had) taken

6. ate
7. given
8. took

9-10. *Sentences will vary.*

Page 155

VERB	PRESENT	PAST	PAST WITH HELPING VERB
1. see	see, sees	saw	(have, has, had) seen
2. do	do, does	did	(have, has, had) done
3. write	write, writes	wrote	(have, has, had) written
4. drive	drive, drives	drove	(have, has, had) driven
5. ring	ring, rings	rang	(have, has, had) rung

6. I rode my horse into the desert. We went up a steep hill. My pony ate grass. I took a look at the moon. It gave back a shimmery light.

REVIEW

Page 156

1. gave
2. gleamed
3. gabbed
4. went
5. gobbled
6. saw
7. slapped
8. said
9. skated
10. smiled
11. I had ridden in a pickup truck.
12. We have gone to the canyon.
13. The trip has taken four days.
14. We had never seen a triple rainbow.
15. They have told us about their trip.

THE VERB *BE*

Page 157

1. is; present
2. were; past
3. am; present
4. are; present
5. was; past
6. You are in the park zoo.
7. He is with you.
8. We were on a field trip.
9. I am next to the roadrunner cage.
10. It was near some tumbleweed.

Page 158

1. am
2. are
3. is
4. are
5. are
6. was
7. were

8. was
9. were
10. were
11. Alejandro is content. The animals are happy at their water hole. They are glad Alejandro is their friend. I am glad, too.

REVIEW

Page 159

	PRESENT	PAST
1.	they have	they had
2.	she is	she was
3.	it says	it said
4.	we go	we went
5.	they are	they were
6.	I am	I was
7.	he does	he did

8. Visitors are welcome at Alejandro's house.
9. It was a small adobe house.
10. Alejandro has a beautiful garden.
11. We rode by in a pickup truck.
12. I am happy in the desert.
13. Some desert animals eat plants.
14. You saw many kinds of plants there.

CONTRACTIONS

Page 160

1. Are not
2. You are
3. it is
4. Do not
5. are not
6. he's
7. they're
8. I'm
9. we're
10. Most people can't climb tall mountains.
11. Mount Everest hasn't proved easy to climb.
12. I wouldn't dare try it.

Page 161

1. couldn't
2. hadn't
3. they're
4. I'm
5. haven't
6. aren't
7. she's
8. we're
9. isn't
10. didn't
11-15. The wind is not kind to rocks. Slowly, it is wearing them down. They are taking on new shapes. Do not be alarmed. You are seeing nature in action.

REVIEW

Page 162

1. (We) are
2. (you) are
3. (It) is
4. (he) is
5. (I) am
6. I'm doing a report about the Himalayas.
7. They're discussed in that book about mountains.
8. You'll learn a lot from my report.
9. I wouldn't want to climb Mount Everest.
10. It's very dangerous.

ADVERBS

Page 163

1. often
2. quickly
3. beautifully
4. today
5. early
6. how
7. when
8. how
9. where

10. when
11-12. *Responses will vary; possible responses are given.*
11. I received a letter yesterday.
12. The postal carrier delivered it here.

Page 164

1. beautifully, write
2. greatly, interest
3. Next, tell
4. clearly, love
5. sometime, Visit
6-10. *Responses will vary.*

REVIEW

Page 165

1. We are going to Texas.
2. That is not a very big armadillo.
3. I think he is very cute.
4. Armadillos do not really write postcards.
5. It is fun to pretend, though.
6. You have not read this book?
7. changes, dramatically; how
8. looked, around; where
9. flew, upward; where
10. took, Then; when
11. flies, quickly; how
12. flew, above; where

COMPARING WITH ADVERBS

Page 166

1. more evenly
2. faster
3. most violently
4. Do comets burn hotter than the Sun?
5. They move more speedily than rocket ships.
6. They are pulled most powerfully of all.
7. The asteroid flew more slowly than the comet.
8. Since the Sun is the closest star, it pulls most forcefully on the earth.

Page 167

ADVERB	COMPARING TWO ACTIONS	COMPARING MORE THAN TWO ACTIONS
1. powerfully	more powerfully	most powerfully
2. loudly	more loudly	most loudly
3. high	higher	highest
4. cleverly	more cleverly	most cleverly
5. quickly	more quickly	most quickly

6-10. *Sentences will vary.*

REVIEW

Page 168

1. brighter
2. goes
3. taken
4. fastest
5. quickly
6. saw
7. told
8. smartest

ADDITIONAL PRACTICE

SENTENCES

Page 170

1. sentence
2. sentence
3. sentence
4. not a sentence
5. sentence
6. sentence
7. not a sentence
8. sentence
9. not a sentence
10. sentence

Page 171

Possible responses are given.

11. sentence
12. She uses hot peppers, tomatoes, and onions.
13. sentence
14. He planted them in milk cartons filled with soil.
15. sentence
16. One morning Victor saw sprouts in the carton.
17. The sprouts grew inside his house for weeks.
18. sentence
19. sentence
20. Victor protected the plants from snails.
21. sentence
22. Before long he had ripe red peppers!
23. sentence
24. They were delicious in tacos and on nachos!
25. Victor's peppers were the winner of the blue ribbon at the fair!

STATEMENTS AND QUESTIONS

Page 172

1. statement
2. not a statement
3. not a statement
4. statement
5. statement
6. question
7. not a question
8. question
9. question
10. not a question

Page 173

Possible responses are given.

11. statement
12. question — She was born in 1867.
13. question — She used the name Nellie Bly.
    OR She did use the name Nellie Bly.
14. question — Women were treated poorly in jails then.
15. statement
16. question — She wrote about what happened.
    OR She did write about what happened.
17. question – People were shocked by her articles.
18. statement
19. question — Cochrane was famous by the time she was twenty-one.
20. question — She decided to travel around the world.
    OR She did decide to travel around the world.
21. statement
22. statement
23. question — Airplanes had already been invented.

EXCLAMATIONS AND COMMANDS

Page 174

1. exclamation
2. not an exclamation
3. exclamation
4. exclamation
5. not an exclamation

6. command
7. not a command
8. command
9. command
10. command

Page 175

11. command
12. exclamation
13. exclamation
14. command
15. command
16. exclamation
17. command
18. exclamation
19. exclamation
20. exclamation
21. exclamation
22. command
23. command
24. exclamation
25. command

PARTS OF A SENTENCE: SUBJECT

Page 176

1. These apples
2. The smell
3. Theo
4. His grandfather
5. The whole family
6. Elena
7. A large red apple
8. The first bite
9. The Green Nursery
10. Each kind

Page 177

Possible responses are given.

11. Mrs. Gonzales
12. Oranges
13. Mosquitoes
14. Eagles
15. The tree's flowers
16. Mint
17. Squirrels and raccoons
18. All plants
19. Some kinds of leaves
20. The honeybee
21. Rosebushes
22. The grass
23. My sister
24. Her dog
25. The park

PARTS OF A SENTENCE: PREDICATE

Page 178

1. announced a contest
2. sponsors the contest
3. displays a jar in its window
4. guesses the number of peanuts in the jar
5. wants to win the grand prize very much
6. needs a new bicycle
7. estimates the size of the jar
8. measures some peanuts
9. can hold about 1,750 peanuts
10. is closest to the correct number.

Page 179

11. She <u>rolls her string into a ball.</u>
12. My aunt <u>ties a new piece of string to the last one on the ball.</u>
13. Each piece <u>makes the ball a little bigger.</u>

14. My aunt's hobby <u>is important to her</u>.
15. People <u>drop pieces of string in odd places</u>.
16. She <u>gathers string from many places</u>.
17. A string ball <u>grows slowly</u>.
18. Francis A. Johnson <u>started a ball of string in 1950</u>.
19. He <u>added to it for 28 years</u>.
20. The ball <u>was almost 13 feet tall by 1978</u>.
21. This amazing ball <u>was 40 feet around</u>.
22. Mr. Johnson <u>became the most famous string collector in the world</u>.
23. The ball of string <u>became famous, too</u>.
24. It <u>was the largest ball of string in history</u>.
25. A hobby <u>can make a person famous</u>.

NOUNS

Page 180
1. friend, flier
2. pal, house
3. girl, moon, day
4. father, pilot
5. man, plane
6. inside, seats
7. family, trip
8. aircraft, fuel
9. group, airport, miles
10. passengers

Page 181
11. The <u>water</u> is cold.
12. The <u>boy</u> stands on the <u>dock</u>.
13. A <u>lifeguard</u> stands nearby.
14. The <u>child</u> dives into the <u>lake</u>.
15. This young <u>camper</u> swims for ten <u>minutes</u>.
16. The <u>counselor</u> later shakes the <u>hand</u> of the <u>swimmer</u>.
17. This <u>test</u> was difficult.
18. Now this <u>student</u> can learn to use a <u>canoe</u>.
19. A <u>paddle</u> lies on the <u>shore</u>.
20. The <u>team</u> practices away from the <u>rocks</u>.
21. The <u>man</u> ties the <u>boat</u> to the <u>dock</u> with <u>rope</u>.

COMMON NOUNS

Page 182
1. person
2. work
3. fellow, sun
4. people, sky
5. bed
6. man, idea, clock
7. machine, bell
8. owner, piece, time
9. chime
10. invention

Page 183
Possible responses are given.
11. The <u>ookpik</u> lives in Australia and Tasmania.
12. It has thick <u>muscles</u> on its <u>legs</u>.
13. Its <u>voice</u> is like the <u>roar</u> of a <u>lion</u>.
14. Its <u>appetite</u> is like that of a <u>pig</u>.
15. <u>Ookpiks</u> live in <u>closets</u> and <u>backyards</u>.
16. They eat <u>tomatoes</u>, <u>cookies</u>, and <u>fries</u>.
17. <u>Ookpiks</u> have <u>whiskers</u> instead of <u>antennae</u>.
18. These furry <u>friends</u> are good <u>protectors</u>.
19. The <u>adult</u> has sharp <u>thorns</u> on its <u>cheeks</u>.
20. It will strike at an <u>octopus</u> with these <u>weapons</u>.

PROPER NOUNS

Page 184
1. Pompeii
2. August
3. Italy
4. Mount Vesuvius
5. Mediterranean Sea
6. Naples
7. Herculaneum
8. Metropolitan Museum
9. Europe
10. Mount Etna

Page 185

11. London, England
12. Europe
13. Africa
14. Jumbo
15. P.T. Barnum
16. Queen Victoria, London Zoo
17. Barnum, North America
18. New York, Chicago, Philadelpia
19. Americans
20. Namibia

SINGULAR AND PLURAL NOUNS

Page 186

1. Sarah, pal
2. sister, land, sea
3. coat, winter
4. Laura, beach
5. January

6. friends, bracelets
7. treasures, boxes
8. books
9. drawings
10. shoes

Page 187

11. coats, eye
12. foxes, hen
13. wires, board, chicken
14. pup
15. girls
16. persons, animals, pets
17. horns, cars
18. hunters, ear
19. airplanes
20. creatures, noise
21. bush

PLURAL NOUNS ENDING IN *IES*

Page 188

1. hobbies
2. pennies, puppies
3. cities
4. countries
5. bullies
6. stories
7. parties
8. comedies
9. pastries
10. jellies

Page 189

11. cities
12. skies
13. daisy
14. lily
15. buddy
16. parties
17. worry
18. families
19. puppies
20. guppy
21. libraries
22. story
23. mystery

IRREGULAR PLURAL NOUNS

Page 190

1. child
2. man
3. woman
4. goose
5. mice
6. ox
7. mouse
8. geese
9. children
10. teeth

Page 191

11. geese
12. tooth
13. men
14. foot
15. oxen
16. women
17. child
18. mouse

POSSESSIVE NOUNS

Page 192

1. room's
2. machine's
3. students'
4. monitor's
5. school's
6. Chester's
7. Joni's
8. friend's
9. user's
10. class's

Page 193

11. That <u>ocean's</u> size surprised her.
12. The <u>sun's</u> light was bright.
13. Vivian took <u>Juni's</u> picture
14. Then Juni took <u>Vivian's</u> picture.
15. The <u>group's</u> task was to observe tide pools.
16. "This <u>one's</u> waves are filling up this pool," Juni said.
17. The two <u>girls'</u> tide pool was busy.
18. A crab interrupted a <u>bug's</u> stroll.
19. The bug ran away from the <u>crab's</u> snapping claws.
20. Vivian counted a <u>starfish's</u> legs.
21. Juni borrowed a <u>friend's</u> pencil.
22. She sketched a <u>creature's</u> shape.
23. Vivian wanted to touch an <u>urchin's</u> spines.
24. She remembered her <u>teacher's</u> instructions, though.
25. "Do not disturb this <u>pool's</u> residents!"

SINGULAR POSSESSIVE NOUNS

Page 194

1. team's
2. no singular possessive noun
3. cap's
4. no singular possessive noun
5. pitcher's
6. shortstop's
7. player's
8. baseman's
9. Daniel's
10. no singular possessive noun

Page 195

11. the family's dinner
12. Dina's mother
13. Her car's engine
14. town's store
15. the day's problem
16. her helmet's strap
17. next town's shop
18. Her mother's stomach
19. her school's parking lot
20. a student's backpack
21. the backpack's cover
22. the owner's name
23. her best friend's backpack

PLURAL POSSESSIVE NOUNS

Page 196

1. trees'
2. no plural possessive noun
3. animals'
4. nuts'
5. oaks'
6. no plural possessive noun
7. squirrels'
8. no plural possessive noun
9. friends'
10. no plural possessive noun

Page 197

11. his neighbors' sidewalks
12. his sisters' laughter
13. two boys' kites
14. the cooks' barbecues
15. the tacos' crispy shells
16. The apartments' residents
17. The parents' pets
18. The pets' behavior
19. The workers' cones
20. The cars' engines
21. The teenagers' radios
22. The dancers' feet

PRONOUNS

Page 198

1. We, you, us, he
2. you, me, I
3. we, he
4. you, I
5. I
6. he, we, she
7. you, her, me, I
8. She, you
9. I, you, I
10. We, you

Page 199

11. She
12. It
13. He
14. It
15. She
16. It
17. They
18. We
19. They
20. It

SINGULAR PRONOUNS

Page 200

1. I
2. She, me
3. I
4. me
5. She, I
6. me
7. you, me, he
8. me, I, her
9. I, I, him
10. I

Page 201

11. He
12. He
13. her
14. him
15. He
16. She
17. It
18. It
19. He

PLURAL PRONOUNS

Page 202

1. We
2. us
3. they
4. we
5. they
6. them
7. them
8. They
9. We
10. us

Page 203

11. We
12. They
13. us
14. They
15. They
16. We
17. We
18. They

SUBJECT PRONOUNS

Page 204

1. We
2. She
3. I
4. It
5. I
6. I
7. It
8. We
9. She
10. we

Page 205

11. It is warm and salty.
12. They live there.
13. He will take pictures under the water.
14. She will develop them.
15. They spot a coral reef beneath the water.
16. It has brightly colored fish around it.
17. He slips into the water.
18. It is there.
19. She shouts a warning.
20. He swims out of the way.
21. He breathes a sigh of relief.
22. They swim by.
23. He photographs the rose-colored fish.
24. It is well-known.
25. Tomorrow they will photograph fish together.

OBJECT PRONOUNS

Page 206

1. him
2. me
3. them
4. them
5. us
6. us
7. them
8. me
9. them
10. it

Page 207

11. it
12. it
13. them
14. it
15. them
16. it
17. it
18. him
19. her
20. them
21. them
22. him
23. me
24. them

ADJECTIVES

Page 208

1. brave
2. five
3. difficult
4. Many
5. fierce, one
6. enough
7. unhappy
8. hungry, thirsty
9. One
10. round

Page 209

11. four, jumps
12. graceful, animal
13. huge, boulder
14. new, roll
15. sudden, movements
16. Three, goats
17. white, coats
18. small, camera
19. five, pictures
20. suspicious, goats
21. long, shadows
22. red, sun
23. heavy, coat
24. long, hike

ADJECTIVES THAT TELL *HOW MANY*

Page 210

1. Several
2. One billion
3. ten
4. Three
5. many
6. two
7. seven, every
8. five
9. one hundred, zero

Page 211

Possible responses are given.

10. four
11. six hundred
12. eighty
13. three hundred
14. two
15. one hundred and eight
16. fourteen
17. three hundred and eighty-one
18. two hundred and forty
19. a thousand
20. fifty-six
21. seventeen
22. forty million
23. many

ADJECTIVES THAT TELL *WHAT KIND*

Page 212

1. interesting
2. new
3. Green
4. large
5. great
6. wooden
7. hidden
8. Tiny
9. silent
10. funny

Page 213

11. tall, grasses
12. dry, earth
13. narrow, road
14. busy, city
15. heavy, sacks
16. large, piece
17. wet, soybeans
18. dark, clouds
19. sharp, stone
20. flat, tire
21. rusty, bolts
22. damaged, tire
23. red, can
24. special, mixture
25. difficult, problem

ARTICLES

Page 214

1. a
2. the, the
3. a
4. An, the
5. An, the
6. An, a
7. A
8. the, the
9. An, the
10. A, the

Page 215

Possible responses are given.

11. A *or* The
12. a *or* the, the
13. a *or* the
14. the
15. A *or* The
16. the *or* a
17. a *or* the
18. the
19. the, the *or* a
20. the, an *or* the
21. the *or* a
22. the *or* an, a *or* the, the
23. the, the *or* an

ADJECTIVES THAT COMPARE: *-ER, -EST*

Page 216

1. rounder
2. bigger
3. no adjective that compares two things
4. faster
5. no adjective that compares two things

6. tallest
7. no adjective that compares more than two things
8. fastest
9. easiest
10. strongest

Page 217

11. faster
12. quicker
13. wisest
14. older
15. thicker
16. longest
17. larger
18. thickest
19. coldest
20. softest
21. smaller
22. smallest

ADJECTIVES THAT COMPARE: *MORE, MOST*

Page 218

1. more rapid
2. more dangerous
3. no adjective that compares two things
4. more common
5. more useful

6. most unusual
7. most powerful
8. no adjectives that compare more than two things
9. most common
10. most healthy

Page 219

11. most
12. more
13. most
14. more
15. most
16. more
17. most
18. more
19. more
20. more
21. most

VERBS

Page 220

1. visits
2. drew
3. painted
4. looked
5. unrolled
6. cut
7. sewed
8. attached
9. formed
10. buzzed

Page 221

Possible responses are given.

11. walks
12. waters
13. bloomed
14. hears
15. swim
16. leaped
17. counted
18. walked

ACTION VERBS

Page 222

1. run
2. jump
3. kick
4. chase
5. escape
6. build
7. digs
8. lays
9. warms
10. hatch

Page 223

Possible responses are given.

11. build
12. fly
13. croak
14. crow
15. swing
16. run
17. jump
18. swim
19. peck
20. bury
21. eat
22. chase
23. produce
24. rest

MAIN VERBS

Page 224

1. planned
2. traveled
3. collected
4. placed
5. searched
6. used
7. stored
8. picked
9. adjusted
10. cleaned

Page 225

11. had visited
12. had arrived
13. have unpacked
14. has raised
15. have helped
16. has traded
17. have provided
18. has gone
19. have walked
20. have enjoyed
21. have cooked
22. have finished

HELPING VERBS

Page 226

1. have
2. has
3. had
4. have
5. have
6. had
7. have
8. have
9. has
10. have

Page 227

11. have lived
12. has recorded
13. had slipped
14. has injured
15. has climbed
16. had helped
17. has provided
18. have liked
19. have used
20. had learned

PRESENT-TIME VERBS

Page 228

1. look
2. sees
3. think
4. surprises
5. moves
6. call
7. knows
8. hunts
9. wraps
10. puts

Page 229

11. The chickens cluck a hello.
12. They stretch their wings.
13. Two hens peck at some grain.
14. A chicken with white feathers gobbles up a slug.
15. The puppy jumps up and down
16. He barks loudly at the chickens.
17. The chickens scatter in the yard.

18. The farm owner greets the chickens with a cheerful wave.
19. She tosses them some broccoli and squash.
20. They nibble the vegetables happily.
21. A large hen scratches at the dirt in the yard.
22. A chick follows her.
23. Two other chickens wander over.
24. A little hen discovers a group of tasty bugs.
25. She shares the bugs with all the other hens.

PAST-TIME VERBS

Page 230

1. sketched
2. traced
3. added
4. jotted
5. totaled
6. checked
7. demonstrated
8. solved
9. praised
10. invented

Page 231

11. sketched
12. marked
13. showed
14. reproduced
15. sawed
16. moved
17. placed
18. arranged
19. completed
20. handed
21. asked

IRREGULAR VERBS

Page 232

1. gave
2. drove
3. eaten
4. went
5. gone
6. came
7. drove
8. given
9. did
10. done

Page 233

11. eaten
12. done
13. came
14. gave
15. did
16. went
17. given
18. gone
19. drove
20. come
21. ate, ate

MORE IRREGULAR VERBS

Page 234

1. took
2. said
3. thought
4. rode
5. ran
6. saw
7. had/has
8. taken
9. thought
10. had

Page 235

11. rode
12. had
13. saw
14. thought
15. had
16. said
17. rode
18. took
19. run
20. saw
21. said
22. taken

THE VERB BE

Page 236

1. is
2. were
3. are
4. am
5. are
6. is
7. is
8. was
9. is
10. are

Page 237

11. is
12. is
13. are
14. are
15. were
16. is
17. was
18. was
19. is
20. were
21. are
22. is
23. are
24. is
25. are

ADVERBS

Page 238

1. yesterday
2. warmly
3. Now
4. ahead
5. swiftly
6. already
7. carefully
8. expertly
9. proudly
10. nearby

Page 239

Possible responses are given.

11. Marco <u>gladly</u> helps his mother.
12. He <u>quickly</u> turns the pages of her music book.
13. Marco's mother plays <u>brightly</u>.
14. <u>Often</u> she stops, though.
15. Marco <u>carefully</u> checks the music book.
16. He finds the next notes <u>carefully</u>.
17. <u>Later</u> he locates the correct piano keys.
18. He <u>heavily</u> touches each key.
19. Marco and his mother <u>usually</u> laugh at mistakes.
20. They sing the words of a song <u>softly</u>.
21. Marco looks <u>around</u> and smiles.
22. A crowd has gathered <u>outside</u>.

To, Too, Two

Page 240

1. two
2. to
3. two
4. too
5. two
6. to
7. to
8. too
9. to
10. to

Page 241

11. I will give her a nice pen, too.
12. Those two things will be a good present.
13. Lisa gave a journal to me last year.
14. I write a page or two in it every day.
15. I took it to my aunt's home this summer.
16. She keeps a journal, too.
17. She read parts of her old journal to me.
18. One part told about her trip to Jamaica.
19. She stayed for two months.
20. My aunt is a good writer and a good cook, too.
21. She gave one of her favorite recipes to me.
22. I cooked it and ate it, too.
23. The two of us enjoyed being together.
24. Soon I will go to Lisa's party.
25. I will walk the two blocks to her house.

YOUR, YOU'RE

Page 242

1. you're
2. your
3. your
4. your
5. your
6. you're
7. Your
8. you're
9. your
10. You're, your

Page 243

11. your
12. you're
13. your
14. You're
15. your
16. You're
17. your
18. You're

ITS, IT'S

Page 244

1. It's
2. its
3. its
4. It's
5. it's
6. It's
7. it's
8. Its
9. it's
10. it's

Page 245

11. A computer stores information in its memory.
12. It's important to know how much memory your computer has.
13. The sentence is correct.
14. You cannot play this game on your computer because its memory is too small.

15. It's time to add some memory to your computer!
16. The sentence is correct.
17. If you put this chip into your computer, you will increase the size of its memory.
18. Let's test your computer to see if its new memory chip is working.
19. Great! It's working perfectly!
20. I like this game because its pictures are so colorful!
21. Now it's time to stop playing the game.
22. Please put the game disk back in its box.
23. Your computer has a screen saver on its main menu.

THEIR, THERE, THEY'RE

Page 246

1. They're
2. their
3. their
4. there
5. their
6. They're
7. There
8. there
9. They're
10. their

Page 247

11. Elephants from Asia are very useful because of their strength and intelligence.
12. They're used as work animals in Thailand.
13. They haul logs through the forest there.
14. It's not easy to prove how good their memories really are.
15. They're able to remember many commands.
16. Dogs use their memory, too.
17. They remember the scent of their owners.
18. They're able to remember where home is, too.
19. Some dogs find their way back home from hundreds of miles away.
20. No one is sure how they're able to do this.
21. Dolphins have large brains for their body size.
22. They're very intelligent animals.
23. Their language is made up of clicks, squeaks, and whistles.

COMMA AFTER INTRODUCTORY WORDS

Page 248

1. "Yes, I have been looking foward to this," said Joni.
2. "Well, do you recognize that person?" said Ben.
3. "No, I don't," Noli replied.
4. "Yes, that is my cousin Jonny," Max replied.
5. "Well, have you ever met him, Joni?"
6. "Well, I must have met him, but I don't remember him," she replied as she looked at the photos.
7. "Yes, let's look at the photos of our trip to New York," Ben said.
8. "No, I would rather see the photos of our visit to the Grand Canyon," Max said.

Page 249

Possible responses are given.

9. Yes,
10. No,
11. No,
12. Well,
13. Well,
14. No,
15. Well,
16. No,
17. Yes,

SERIES COMMA

Page 250

1. My sister, my parents, and my grand-parents all went to see the palace there.
2. In the palace we saw a throne room, a swimming pool, and some guest rooms.
3. Our tour guide spoke French, German, and English.
4. The palace rooms were decorated with stones, rugs, and jewels.
5. People came long ago from India, China, and Europe to bring the sultan gifts.
6. We were hot, tired, and hungry after the tour.

7. At lunch we had lamb, grapes, and baklava.
8. Then we went to the market, which was busy, loud, and colorful.
9. The apricots, figs, and dates all looked delicious.
10. That evening we watched boats, barges, and ferries glide past the city.

Page 251

11. We were having lamb chops, mashed potatoes, and peas.
12. Lightning flashed, thunder crashed, and rain began falling.
13. The wind whistled, howled, and moaned.
14. Thunder rumbled, crashed, and boomed.
15. The windows rattled, the screen door banged, and the lights all went out.
16. Lightning jumped, leaped, and danced across the sky.
17. I shivered, moaned, and cried.
18. The house was damp, dark, and scary.
19. My mother brought out a flashlight, a candle, and matches.
20. Mom, Dad, and I did not feel like eating.
21. We told jokes, played games, and sang songs.
22. The lightning, thunder, and rain finally stopped.
23. Then the lights, the air conditioner, and the radio came back on.